THE HARDER A WIFE WORKS, THE CUTER SHE LOOKS

NEW HOLLAND

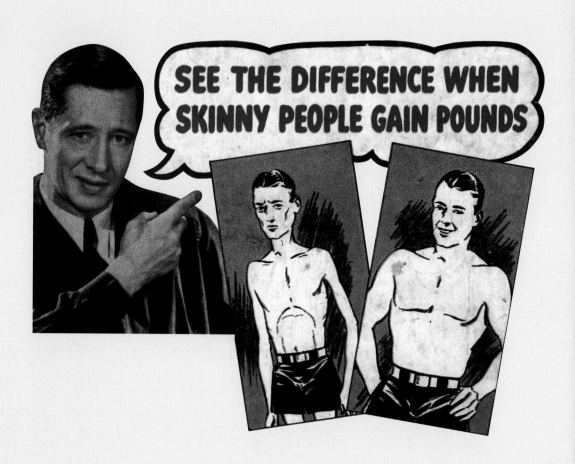

Contents

Introduction

So what *does* the doctor smoke? Pretty much anything, if you believe the adverts in this book! Yes, when these doctors aren't busy telling us to drink whisky and eat sweets, they're falling over themselves to endorse their favourite cigarettes. Sometimes elbowing sports stars out of the way to do so ...

It's not just the way the medical and sporting professions were used to sell unsuitable products that seems strange to modern sensibilities – can you imagine a modern dieting aid advert headed 'Fat Folk'? Or even an advert for bread that features a huge, growling, scary wolf?

And if you think the means of selling is odd – look at the products themselves! They range from a belt that electrocutes its wearer to provide 'vigour' to a 'chin reducer and beautifier' contraption that looks more like a torture device.

Funny and ridiculous as they undoubtedly are, deliberate humour doesn't play

a big part in these adverts, maybe because it's only in retrospect that we can see

that Dri-Poo for the hair might not be the most savoury of names, or that a horse

exercise machine (guaranteed satisfaction) might find its real market in sexually-

frustrated Victorian housewives.

But perhaps the real reason the adverts in this book make us laugh out loud is because they come from eras with completely different ideas and values from ours – where pesticide-covered oranges were a good

thing and sunlamps were genuinely used to ward off the flu in children.

And that's the warning these adverts should give us. We may think we're more

sophisticated now, but under all the gloss of modern marketing, has much really

changed? Next time you're convinced you need the latest must-have product, look

back at this book and beware!

Drink for health

Alcohol has always been used for medicinal purposes, but you don't get many adverts nowadays that sell it as a curative first and foremost, before the 'fun and relaxation' element, or the 'get out of your tree and forget the mess you've made of your miserable life' one. Still, it's a lot easier to justify buying whisky by the caseload if it's your medicine cabinet you're re-stocking, rather than the drinks one. Not that the people in these adverts are a great recommendation for the health-giving properties of booze – they're mostly either decrepit or boss-eyed …

1900
M. D. Daly and Sons Advert

Pouring it through a funnel doesn't make it medicine,
but you can't blame the old boy for trying.

**1910s
Hall's Wine Advert**

This advert might
have a fair enough
claim if it wasn't for
her cross eyes.

**1920s
Whiteway's Advert**

An apple a day
keeps the doctor
away. And
apparently the
same is true if it's
an alcoholic apple.
How convenient!

**1930s
Dewar's Advert**

Wonder if there's a
similar cure for
bird flu? Fingers
crossed!

**1900s
Newball and
Mason Advert**

Mason's essence is
non-alcoholic,
which is just as well
if you serve it at
kids' parties by the
gallon.

**1933
Dewar's Advert**

Now that's the kind
of doctor's advice
I like!

1950s Seagers Advert

After drinking a mixture of egg and wine, swinging her around like that might not be the best idea.

**1958
Rheingold Advert**

Madelyn loves a beer before she jumps in her car. Just hope that dog moves out of the way quick enough.

DRUNKENNESS CURED.

It is now within the reach of Every Woman to Save the Drunkard—A Free Trial Package of a Marvellous Home Remedy Posted to All Who Write for it.

Can be Given in Tea, Coffee, or Food, thus absolutely and secretly Curing the Patient in a Short Time without his knowledge.

There is a cure for drunkenness which has shed a radiance into thousands of hitherto desolate firesides. It does its work so silently and surely that while the devoted wife, sister, or daughter looks on, the drunkard is reclaimed even against his will and without his knowledge or co-operation. The Company who have this grand remedy will send a sample free to all who will write for it. Enough of this remedy is posted in this way to show how it is used in tea, coffee, or food, and that it will cure the dreaded habit quietly and permanently.

A lady residing in Manchester used the remedy as described above, and her experience, told in her own words, will quite likely interest all women deeply. Mrs.—— says: "Yes, I used Antidipso without my husband's knowledge, and completely cured him. He was a hard drinker, a good man when sober, but for years I lived in fear and dread, shame and despair, poverty and disgrace. How shall I tell other women about it? Is it not a wonderful thing that a woman can take matters in her own hands and stamp out this dreadful curse to the home? I am glad you are going to publish my experience, for then I know it will reach hundreds of other poor souls, and they will cure their husbands just as I cured mine. I am so grateful for the marvellous changes that have come into my life that I just feel I would do anything to let every wife and mother know what a blessing Antidipso is. I honestly believe it will cure any drunkard, no matter how far down he may have fallen.—Faithfully yours, Mrs.——"
(Full address sent to *bona-fide* applicants.)

Hundreds of others are reported, even the worst cases where the habit seems to have blotted out the last remaining spark of self-respect. Tears and prayers are of no use. Pleading, pledges, loss of social or business position are unavailing to stem the tide of absolute depravity.

This famous remedy has reunited thousands of scattered families; it has saved thousands of men to social and business prominence and public respect; has guided many a young man into the right road to fortune; has saved the father, the brother, the son, and in many cases the wife and daughter, too. Such a godsend to the home should be known to everyone. Upon application to the **Ward Chemical Co., 10, Century House, Regent Street, London, W.,** they will post a free package of the remedy to you, securely sealed in a plain wrapper, also full directions how to use it, books, testimonials from hundreds who have been cured, and everything needed to aid you in saving those near and dear to you from a life of degradation and ultimate poverty and disgrace. Send for a free trial to-day. It will brighten the rest of your life.

**1890s
Antidipso Advert**

And if you're still not convinced that drink is good for your health, why not try Antidipso? Just slip it in his tea and watch him jump back on that wagon!

You too can look like a model

Inner beauty is for ugly people. It's a superficial world we live in so if you want to make the most of what nature gave you, then take a look at the informative adverts that follow. Yes, certain gorgeousness awaits you once you've strapped one of these not-at-all-cumbersome contraptions around your head, smothered your face with one of these categorically non-poisonous lotions or swallowed a few of these oh-so-tasty-sounding tablets. Want to lose weight? Beef up your muscles? Grow some hair? Not a problem; it's all easily within your reach if you just send a prompt cheque to the address given …

**1890s
Gillette advert**

Aah, is there a lovelier sight in the world than a baby happily waving a razor blade around in its chubby little fist?

CURVES OF YOUTH

will be yours if you will

"Pull the Cords"

Gives the
Flesh the
Resiliency
and
Freshness
of
Youth

PROF.
MACK'S

Chin Reducer

and

Beautifier

Prevents
Double
Chins

Effaces
Double
Chins

Reduces
Enlarged
Glands

The only mechanism producing a concentrated, continuous massage of the chin and neck, dispelling flabbiness of the neck and throat, restoring a rounded contour to thin, scrawny necks and faces, bringing a natural, healthy color to the cheeks, effacing lines and wrinkles. Price only $10. What better investment could be made? Sent postpaid immediately.

Free Booklet

—giving valuable information on how to treat double chin and enhance facial beauty will be sent on request. Write at once to

Prof. Eugene Mack

507 Fifth Ave.   **Suite 1004**   **New York**

**1890s
Curves of Youth
Advert**

Much as this looks
like a torture
device, it is actually
the secret to a
youthful look.
A youthful horse,
that is.

**1890s
Madame Rowley's
Toilet Mask
Advert**

Hannibal Lecter has nothing on this woman. Yet apparently the Toilet Mask 'cannot be detected by the closest scrutiny'. *Unless* you happen to notice the huge straps covering her head and the weird skin, of course.

MADAME ROWLEY'S TOILET MASK.

TOILET MASK
OR
FACE GLOVE.

The following are the claims made for Madame Rowley's Toilet Mask, and the grounds on which it is recommended to ladies for Beautifying, Bleaching, and Preserving the Complexion:

TOILET MASK
OR
FACE GLOVE.

First—The Mask is Soft and Flexible in form, and can be Easily Applied and Worn without Discomfort or Inconvenience.

Second—It is durable, and does not dissolve or come asunder, but holds its original mask shape.

Third—It has been Analyzed by Eminent Scientists and Chemical Experts, and pronounced Perfectly Pure and Harmless.

Fourth—With ordinary care the Mask will last for years, and its VALUABLE PROPERTIES Never Become Impaired.

Fifth—The Mask is protected by letters patent, and is the only Genuine article of the kind.

Sixth—It is Recommended by Eminent Physicians and Scientific Men as a SUBSTITUTE FOR INJURIOUS COSMETICS.

Seventh—The Mask is a Natural Beautifier, for Bleaching and Preserving the Skin and Removing Complexional Imperfections.

Eighth—Its use cannot be detected by the closest scrutiny, and it may be worn with perfect privacy, if desired.

Ninth—The Mask is sold at a moderate price, and is to be PURCHASED BUT ONCE.

Tenth—Hundreds of dollars uselessly expended for cosmetics, lotions, and like preparations, may be saved its possessor.

Eleventh—Ladies in every section of the country are using the Mask with gratifying results.

Twelfth—It is safe, simple, cleanly, and effective for beautifying purposes, and never injures the most delicate skin.

Thirteenth—While it is intended that the Mask should be Worn During Sleep, it may be applied WITH EQUALLY GOOD RESULTS at any time to suit the convenience of the wearer.

Fourteenth—The Mask has received the testimony of well-known society and professional ladies, who proclaim it to be the greatest discovery for beautifying purposes ever vouchsafed to womankind.

The Toilet Mask (or Face Glove) in position to the face.
TO BE WORN THREE TIMES IN THE WEEK

COMPLEXION BLEMISHES

May be hidden imperfectly by cosmetics and powders, but can only be removed permanently by the Toilet Mask. By its use every kind of spots, impurities, roughness, etc., vanish from the skin, leaving it soft, clear, brilliant, and beautiful. It is harmless, costs little, and saves its user money. It prevents and removes wrinkles, and is both a complexion preserver and beautifier. Famous Society Ladies, actresses, belles, etc., use it.

VALUABLE ILLUSTRATED TREATISE, WITH PROOFS AND PARTICULARS.
—MAILED FREE BY—

TOILET MASK
OR
FACE GLOVE.
[1887]

Send for Descriptive Treatise.

THE TOILET MASK COMPANY,
1164 BROADWAY,
NEW YORK.
Mention this paper when you Write.

Send for Descriptive Treatise.

TOILET MASK
OR
FACE GLOVE.

A PERFECT LOOKING NOSE

CAN EASILY BE YOURS.

Trados Model No. 25— British Patent—corrects all ill-shaped noses quickly, painlessly, permanently and comfortably at home (diseased cases excepted). It is the only adjustable, safe and guaranteed patent device that will actually give you a perfect looking nose. Over 89,000 satisfied users (ladies, gentlemen and children). For years recommended by physicians. 17 years' experience in manufacturing Nose Shapers is at your service. Write for free booklet which tells you how to obtain a perfect looking nose

M. TRILETY, *Specialist*, **Rex House, D.542, 45, Hatton Garden, London, E.C.1.**

1900s
M. Trilety Advert

If only all those people who've had nose jobs
had known about this amazing device – so easy!
And so attractive!

1900s
Jonteel Advert

It's always a worry,
that you'll put on
your night cream
and wake up with a
full-grown beard.
But fortunately for
this lady, Jonteel
'will not grow hair
on the face'. Phew!

**1900s
Aspinall's Advert**

It's slightly
unnerving when
a product has to
tell you it won't
poison you.

FAT FOLK

Should take **FELL'S REDUCING TABLETS.**

Registered by Government.

A Remarkable Remedy

That Reduces Weight 28 lb. a month.

Every person who is suffering from too much fat can easily be reduced in weight by this new and remarkable remedy that quickly removes all superfluous fat in either sex at the rate of **7 LB. A WEEK.**

It is guaranteed to **Reduce Weight a Pound a Day** without the slightest inconvenience. Do not be afraid of evil consequences. It is a vegetable treatment, is perfectly safe, and gives such a degree of comfort as to astonish those who have panted and perspired under the weight of excessive fat. It improves the breathing, gives the heart freedom, takes off the big stomach, enables the lungs to expand naturally, and you feel a hundred times better the first day you try this wonderful **HOME TREATMENT.**

"Getting Fleshier Every Day."

Lost 40 lb. Lady —— writes: "Since taking your tablets I am reduced in weight 40 lb."

Thousands of Testimonials sent on request.

FREE Just to prove how effective, pleasant, and safe this remedy is to reduce weight, we are sending free trials. If you want one send us your name and address and two stamps to pay for postage. It costs you nothing to try it. Each box is sent in a plain sealed package, with no advertisement on it to indicate what it contains. Correspondence strictly confidential. Address: **Fell Formula Association, 20 Century House, Regent Street, London, W.**

1903
Fell's Reducing Tablets Advert

'Takes off the big stomach'. Perhaps Ryvita might like to borrow that for their adverts?

YES!

DRI-POO

Certainly Improves My Hair!

Have you tried it yet?

The New Way to Fluff and Clean the Hair

DRI-POO is a delightful preparation and so good for the hair. Excess oil, dandruff, "dirt" and all foreign matter instantly respond to a Dri-Poo treatment. Use it as often as you wish. It is harmless. Just loosen the hair with your fingers, fill with Dri-Poo and brush out. That's all. And the result is hair sweetly clean, fluffy and in the best dressing condition.

We will send a small size can of Dri-Poo to your home postpaid for 25 cents or 50 cents for the large size, if you will mention the name of your merchant.

Our booklet, "The Crown of Beauty," which we will send free on request for the name of your merchant, tells how to prevent discolored, faded, brittle and falling hair, and also gives valuable hints about dressing the hair.

J. J. WITTWER   **Seattle. Wash.**

**1920s
Dri-Poo Advert**

Oh dear, this is an unfortunate name. Or maybe it's not and they really are suggesting rubbing desiccated crap in your hair.

**1920s
Vreeland Advert**

This man is frightening. Do not send him your address. No hair is worth it.

If I can't grow hair for you in 30 days
you get this check

By Alois Merke
Founder of the Famous Merke Institute
Fifth Avenue, New York

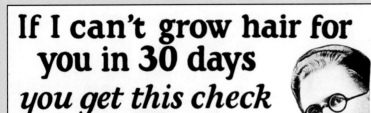

IS that clear? If my treatment fails to grow new hair in 30 days—if it doesn't end dandruff—if it doesn't stop falling hair—simply tell me so and I will immediately mail you a check for every penny you paid me.

No matter how fast your hair is falling out—no matter how much of it is gone—this offer stands.

I don't ask you any questions in case you are not satisfied with my treatment. I don't even ask you in what way my treatment failed.

If you are not absolutely delighted with the results you get—if my treatment fails to do any one of the things I say it will do—simply let me know and I will send you by return mail a check refunding every penny of your money. And, remember, you alone are the judge of whether my treatment works or not.

Why This Offer?

How am I able to make this amazing offer? The answer is simple. My system of hair growth is founded upon a recent scientific discovery. I have found during many years of research and experience in the Merke Institute, Fifth Avenue, New York, that in most cases of baldness the hair roots are NOT dead. They are merely dormant—asleep!

It is an absolute waste of time—a shameful waste of money—to try to penetrate to these dormant roots with ordinary oils, massages and tonics which merely treat the surface skin. You wouldn't expect to make a tree grow by rubbing growing fluid on the bark—get at the roots. And that is just what my scientific system does. It penetrates below the surface of the scalp. It stimulates the dormant roots.

It awakens them. The tiny capillaries begin to pump Nature's own nourishment into them. Hair begins to grow again. It takes on body and color. No artificial hair foods—no rubbing. And here's the wonderful thing about this system. It is simple. You can use it at home—in any home that has electricity—easily—without the slightest discomfort.

Free Booklet Tells All

Thousands of men and women have been treated successfully at the Merke Institute. Hundreds daily are getting amazing results with this easier, less expensive "at home" system of hair growth. Now, I do not say that all cases of loss of hair are curable. There are some that nothing in the world can help. Yet so many men and women write in daily about the wonderful results that I gladly make this offer. Try this remarkable treatment for 30 days. Then, if you're not delighted, simply return the treatment and you will get your money back instantly and without question. There's no room here to tell you all about your hair and about the amazing contract I offer you. But I will be glad to tell you all about it if you are interested. Just mail the coupon and I will send you, in plain wrapper, without cost, a wonderfully interesting booklet that describes in detail the system that is proving a boon to thousands in this and other countries. Mail this coupon and the free Booklet will reach you by return mail. Allied Merke Institutes, Inc., Dept. 551, 512 Fifth Avenue, New York City.

**Allied Merke Institutes, Inc.,
Dept. 551, 512 Fifth Ave.,
New York City.**

Please send me in plain wrapper—without cost or obligation—a copy of your free book, "The New Way to Grow Hair," describing the Merke System.

Name...

Address...

City.................... State............

HERE'S PROOF!
Hair Coming Back

"Having used your Thermocap Treatment for 30 days, find a new growth of hair coming back on bald spot. It is growing in very fine. The Thermocap is a treatment that everyone who is losing his hair should buy."
—*G. H. C., Portland, Me.*

Dandruff Leaves Entirely

"I want to tell you how wonderful your treatment is. The first week my dandruff left entirely, and by the third week a new growth of hair could be seen all over my head."—*Mrs. H. S., Port Angeles, Wash.*

Partly Bald for 10 Years

"I have been partly bald for the last 10 years, and have used your treatment four weeks to date, but I can already see a new crop of hair coming in."—*J. A. K., Anderson, Ind.*

**1920s
Alois Merke
Advert**

Alois is going to be a busy (not to mention bushy) man – growing hair for all his customers …

**1930s
Perihel Advert**

Does your child need 'vitaminising'? Have you tried cooking her under a sunlamp for a few hours?

For 1940 — Be Fit & Slim

Every woman wants to look better, to feel better in the year ahead. Slenderness is the way to health, beauty and fitness. A couple of Bile Beans taken nightly enables you to 'slim while you sleep'— surely and safely.

These fine vegetable pills do more than disperse unwanted fat— they purify and enrich the blood, tone up the entire system and make you feel better in health in every way.

So start with Bile Beans to-night and make sure of looking and feeling your best in 1940.

By Taking BILE BEANS

SOLD EVERYWHERE

BRAND PILLS

**1940s
Bile Beans Advert**

Mmm … bile beans. How very tempting. And if they repeat on you afterwards, they'll taste exactly the same.

**1940s
Ironized Yeast
Tablets Advert**

Thanks for that, Gil.
Looks a little bit
like you've just
drawn two made-
up pictures – one
skinny and one
beefy – but I'm sure
that's not the case.

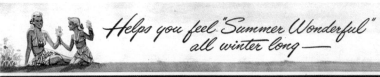

NEW, SUPER-POWERED 575 WATT

Sperti
2-in-1 lamp brings you ultra-violet or infra-red

AT THE SNAP OF A SWITCH

Just flip the switch to the center for ultra-violet . . . to the right for soothing, pain-relieving infra-red

What a welcome you'll give it . . . this new wonder lamp by the makers of famous Sperti Sunlamps. The Sperti 2-in-1 Lamp is really two lamps in one, with twin effectiveness. Brings you the benefits of ultra-violet, right in your own home, during dull winter months. And, at the flick of a switch, it provides powerful, penetrating infra-red to help soothe away muscular aches and pains. *Available now* at all leading stores. See it. Ask for a FREE demonstration. An amazing value. Only $48.50*.

EVERYONE IN THE FAMILY WILL USE IT!

The Sperti 2-in-1 Lamp operates on AC or DC. Genuine high-intensity mercury arc. Streamlined stand adjusts to any height or position. Designed by a world-famous scientist. Approved by Underwriters' Laboratories.

NEW Sperti H-300 SUNLAMP TANS FASTER THAN FLORIDA SUNSHINE

Super-powered 600 watts! . . . Operates on AC or DC . . . Tans any skin the sun itself will tan . . . Genuine high-intensity mercury arc. New scientifically-constructed electro-polished reflector provides up to 50% more reflective power . . . Completely adjustable stand . . . Homerized finish with satin chrome trim . . . Designed by a world-famous scientist . . . Approved by Underwriters' Laboratories. Only $64.50.

I Also see the powerful 560-Watt Sperti Portable Sunlamp, Model P-100. Tans fast. Compact as a camera. Only $37.50*)

Complete with goggles and full instructions for use. Automatic timer, at slight additional cost.

PRODUCTS OF *Sperti* INC. CINCINNATI 12, OHIO • RESEARCH • DEVELOPMENT • MANUFACTURING

Copyright 1947, Sperti, Inc.

**1947
Sperti Advert**

'If I close my eyes tight enough, mum might stop giving me skin cancer.'

**1970s
Cabot Sloane
Advert**

Transformation indeed! She's not only changed from 'fat and lonely' to 'slim and desirable', she's also gained a third dimension and no longer resembles Chewbacca.

Smoking is good for you

Smoking gets a bad rap these days, what with the lung cancer, the hacking cough and the bad breath … Not so in the late 19th and early 20th centuries. Back then, cigarettes were everyone's favourite friends. Doctors, dentists, sportsmen, singers and film stars: they were queuing up to lend their names to the cigarette companies' ad campaigns. Each brand was keen to stress that their cigarettes were the ones to relieve your hoarse voice, prevent you from binge eating and stop your teeth resembling Shane MacGowan's. When adverts featured glamorous women, athletic men and kindly old doctors, who wouldn't be convinced?

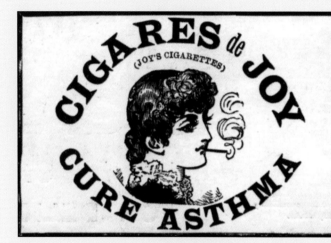

JOY'S CIGARETTES afford immediate relief in cases of **ASTHMA, WHEEZING,** AND **WINTER COUGH,** and a little perseverance will effect a permanent cure. Universally recommended by the most eminent physicians and medical authors. Agreeable to use, certain in their effects, and harmless in their action, they may be safely smoked by ladies and children.

All Chemists and Stores, box of 35, 2s. 6d., or post free from WILCOX & CO., 239, OXFORD STREET, LONDON, W.

1890s
Cigares de Joy Advert

You might think a child with asthma needs an inhaler, but apparently not – Joy's cigarettes were great for kids!

Pass a <u>B.D.V.</u> CIGARETTE between your finger and thumb and notice how perfectly the Tobacco is packed in it.

The long strands of tobacco are perfectly compressed to admit of perfect combustion ; there are no loose bits of tobacco to irritate the palate or the throat ; and there is that full measure of leaf which gives full value and full weight.

B.D.V. Cigarettes

can be Smoked All Day.

They are perfectly pure and dustless, and their flavour and aroma can be enjoyed without palling on the palate.

Buy a tin to-day and test their superb quality.

Enquiries from the Colonies and abroad should be addressed to Export Department, 60-62, Commercial Street, London, E.

2/2 Sold in Tins of 100.

If you are unable to obtain them at your Tobacconist's, send 2/2 for sample tin of 100, post free, to the manufacturers—

GODFREY PHILLIPS & SONS,
112, Commercial Street, London, E.

**1910s
BDV Advert**

BDV cigarettes 'can be smoked all day' – although surely that interferes with other harmless activities? What about constant gin drinking?

**1910s
Craven A Advert**

Ah, those were the days, when doctors recommended not just 5-a-day of your fruit and veg but also 20-a-day of his favourite fags.

What the Doctor Smokes

The doctor's choice in tobacco is CRAVEN Mixture, and he is supported in that choice by the verdict of the greatest medical journal in the world—

"The Lancet"

which published on August 24th, 1912, an analytical report showing that of all well-known tobaccos CRAVEN is unmistakably the purest and best, the smoke of other well-known tobaccos yielding **7 to 10 times, and some tobaccos 16 times, as much nicotine** as that found in CRAVEN. Therefore the doctor smokes and should recommend CRAVEN Mixture as the **best** for **health.**

The purity and sweetness of CRAVEN are due to the special process possessed only by Carreras, Ltd., and by which all impurities and crude nicotine are removed.

CRAVEN MIXTURE is made under the same formula as when immortalised by J. M. Barrie as "Arcadia" in my "Lady Nicotine," and it contains nothing but pure tobacco.

On sale all over the world. In cartridges or loose in tins 2 oz. 1/3
CARRERAS, LTD. (Est. 1788), Arcadia Works, City Rd., London, E.C. & Montreal, Canada.   West-end Depot: 7, Wardour St. Leicester Sq. London, W.

PUNCH, OR THE LONDON CHARIVARI.—December 4, 1929.
xv
IT'S BETTER TO BE FIT THAN FAT
Don't eat between meals
EATING between meals causes fat, and fat destroys your waistline — your fitness—your energy. Here's a simple pleasant way to overcome the craving for between-meal bites — it's the Kensitas way. Every time you have the temptation to eat between meals — don't do it — smoke a Kensitas instead. There's a mellow satisfaction in the appetising aroma of a Kensitas. You'll be delighted to see how quickly the Kensitas way eliminates the desire to eat between meals. Try it — you'll like it!
MANUFACTURED BY THE KENSITAS PRIVATE PROCESS
10 for 6d – 20 for 1/-
"As good as really good cigarettes can be"
"Your Kensitas Cigarettes Sir"
REAL VIRGINIA

1929
Kensitas Advert

Not a bit of advice you'll find in most modern diet books.

**1930s
Lucky Strike
Advert**

Sex sells. And, er,
so do doctors by
the sound of it.

**1930s
Lucky Strike
Advert**

What the ad
doesn't mention is
that Carole is
singing baritone in
a Welsh Miners'
Choir.

1932
Murad advert

It's important for a company to identify its target market – Murad obviously thought its was 'careless drivers who don't like confrontation'. Seems a little narrow, but Murad knows best …

PUNCH, OR THE LONDON CHARIVARI.—December 9, 1931.   xiii

**1930s
Kensitas Advert**

Don't you just hate the man who dares to cough when surrounded by smokers? How rude!

**1930s
Lucky Strike
Advert**

Who'd have
thought that
snacking between
meals was the
downfall of this
aspiring hurdler? If
only he'd had a
40-a-day habit.

**1930s
Cooltipt Advert**

Who knew wool
was so effective?
That must be why
you don't see
sheep with
smokers' coughs.

1940s
Camels Advert

Perhaps the most worrying thing about this ad is what the doctor with the microscope is looking at – and whether that particular patient's test results revealed they were in fact made of fag ash...

NOTED THROAT SPECIALISTS REPORT on *30-Day Test of Camel smokers…*

Not one single case of throat irritation *due to smoking* CAMELS!

Yes, these were the findings of noted throat specialists after a total of 2,470 weekly examinations of the throats of hundreds of men and women who smoked Camels— and only Camels—for 30 consecutive days.

FRED ASTAIRE reports:
"I MADE MY OWN 30-DAY MILDNESS TEST. IT'S **CAMELS** FOR ME FROM NOW ON!"

Start your own 30-Day Camel MILDNESS Test Today!

The inimitable Fred Astaire has been King of the Dance for as long as most theatre-goers can remember. Fred calls time for a Camel as he works out a new ballroom routine at the famed Fred Astaire Dance Studios.

"Camels agree with my throat!"

R. J. Reynolds Tobacco Co.
Winston-Salem, N. C.

1940s Camel Advert

If Fred's 30-day mildness test convinced him, that's good enough for his glamorous assistant!

**1940s
Viceroy Advert**

Never? Perhaps
they mean stain
them white ...

"I'm going to grow a hundred years old!"

...and possibly she may—for the amazing strides of medical science have added years to life expectancy

● It's a fact—a warm and wonderful fact— that this five-year-old child, or your own child, has a life expectancy almost a whole decade longer than was her mother's, and a good 18 to 20 years longer than that of her grandmother. Not only the expectation of a longer life, but of a life by far healthier. Thank medical science for that. Thank your doctor and thousands like him... toiling ceaselessly, often with little or no public recognition... that you and yours may enjoy a longer, better life.

According to a recent Nationwide survey:

More Doctors smoke Camels

than any other cigarette!

NOT ONE but three outstanding independent research organizations conducted this survey. And they asked not just a few thousand, but 113,597, doctors from coast to coast to name the cigarette they themselves preferred to smoke.

The answers came in by the thousands... from general physicians, diagnosticians, surgeons—yes, and nose and throat specialists too. The most-named brand was Camel.

If you are not now smoking Camels, try them. Compare them critically. See how the full, rich flavor of Camel's costlier tobaccos suits your taste. See how the cool mildness of a Camel suits your throat. Let your "T-Zone" tell you (*see right*).

THE "T-ZONE" TEST WILL TELL YOU

The "T-Zone"—T for taste and T for throat—is your own proving ground for any cigarette. Only your taste and throat can decide which cigarette tastes best to you... how it affects your throat. On the basis of the experience of many, many millions of smokers, we believe Camels will suit your "T-Zone" to a "T"

R. J. Reynolds Tobacco Co.,
Winston-Salem, N. C.

CAMELS Costlier Tobaccos

CAMEL
TURKISH & DOMESTIC BLEND
CIGARETTES

1940s Camel Advert

Notice how the top section of this advert has nothing to do with the bottom? But maybe she will live forever... as long as she stays away from those cigarettes her doctor's so keen on.

**1940
New White Owl
Advert**

So that's where Tim Henman's been going wrong – not as many cigars in his training plan.

Back from Havana :—

OWL: Hello, Fred—did you have a good time in Cuba?

PERRY: Yes . . . thank you. I'm only sorry I had to leave that part of the world so soon.

OWL: Did you smoke any Havana cigars while you were down there?

PERRY: That's a treat I never miss when I'm in Cuba. That Havana taste suits me.

FRED PERRY APPROVES HAVANA FLAVOR OF NEW WHITE OWL

OWL: Do us a favor, will you? Try this *new* White Owl Cigar and tell us what you think of it.

PERRY: Sure thing—but I warn you I'm finicky about cigars. (*After several puffs*.) Say, that's something, now. There's Havana flavor for you . . . mild, too!

FRED PERRY, internationally famous tennis star, recently returned from an exhibition tour of Cuba. We interviewed him when he arrived in New York. Knowing that he smoked cigars and that he would be fresh from the home of Havana flavor, we asked him to check the *new* White Owl for Havana flavor.

The *new* Blended-with-Havana White Owl does have a rich Havana flavor—hundreds of thousands of smokers will go along with Fred Perry on that. And the fact that you now can get this preferred cigar taste in a good 5¢ cigar accounts for *new* White Owl sales record. Are you missing out on this cigar "find" of the year?

NOW BLENDED WITH HAVANA!

Try a **NEW WHITE OWL**—*Today* 5¢

See how the new White Owls are made—New York World's Fair, 1940

Copyright, 1940, by General Cigar Co., Inc.

STRAMONIUM CIGARETTES HELPFUL IN

ASTHMA

as reported in the British Medical Journal, August 15, 1959

Noted allergist reinvestigates an old treatment for bronchial asthma

For about 150 years Europeans have inhaled smoke from burning stramonium leaves to relieve asthmatic attacks.

Now a noted allergist reports in the British Medical Journal that results of controlled studies leave no doubt that inhaling stramonium (atropine*) smoke has a beneficial effect on the function of the lungs in bronchial obstruction.

The results indicate that smoking stramonium cigarettes has a definite place in the treatment of asthma, increasing the vital capacity and giving a feeling of relief, without unpleasant side effects. In many cases during the controlled study the patients voluntarily commented on their increased ease of breathing.

Stramonium cigarettes have been manufactured by R. Schiffmann Co. for more than 80 years and have been *available without prescription in every drug store* throughout the U.S. and Canada under the name of ASTHMADOR. These cigarettes contain no tobacco and are not habit forming.

ASTHMADOR is also sold in pipe mixture or as aromatic incense powder. Sufferers from bronchial asthma will almost invariably find relief, as indicated in this report.

Atropine is the alkaloid of stramonium.

1960s Asthmador Advert

Stramonium is now known to be toxic – surely being poisoned would be classed as an 'unpleasant side effect'?

**1975
Tipalet Advert**

An unusual pulling
technique, this one.
Or perhaps that's
chloroform he's
blowing at her
and she'll be out
in seconds?

Blow in her face and she'll follow you anywhere.

Hit her with tangy Tipalet Cherry. Or rich, grape-y Tipalet
Burgundy. Or luscious Tipalet Blueberry. It's Wild!
Tipalet. It's new. Different. Delicious in taste and in aroma.
A puff in her direction and she'll follow you, anywhere.
Oh yes...you get smoking satisfaction without inhaling smoke.

Smokers of America,
do yourself a flavor.
Make your next
cigarette a
Tipalet.

New from Muriel.   About 5 for 25¢.

You are what you eat: a donut

Healthy eating is nothing new. It's just that back in the first half of the 20th century, 'healthy eating' meant stuffing your face with sweets and fizzy drinks – hooray! Sounds like much more fun than boring old fruit and vegetables ...

But while a lot of these brands are healthy-enough foods that are still going strong today, their advertising has grown up a lot in the last 70 or so years – you won't see many snarling wolves or sad and raggedy-looking urchins in modern adverts, more's the pity.

**1890s
Grove's Advert**

In the 1890s, being as fat as a pig was obviously something to be envied. Why isn't that the case any more, alas?

1890s
Hovis Advert

It's an interesting approach from Hovis to use a huge growling wolf to sell their bread. Wonder why it's not more common?

1911
Quaker Oats Advert

The dirty, scraggy-looking one on the left or the goblin-ears child on the right?

1917
Allenburys Foods
Advert

Same boy aged 32 years: undergoing therapy after having embarrassing baby snaps shown to world.

**1920s
Dr Bundensen
Advert**

Well? Do you? Best have another KitKat Chunky, just to be on the safe side.

**1931
Skipper's Advert**

Did his mother warn her about the 'repeating'? Perhaps that's why she's so keen on filling him with sardines.

**1930s
Libby's Advert**

Gee whiz, how fun is breakfast in this house? I'm guessing it's not the 'sauerkraut' flavour that he's drinking, or he wouldn't look nearly so happy.

**1940s
White Castle
Advert**

The entertainer of the 1940s had it right – why slave over a hot stove when you can buy your dinner in a sack?

1942
Skinless Advert

This chap loves his
sausage sandwich!
Plus eating
sausages to defeat
Hitler sounds a lot
easier than the
other option ...

FOOD POWER will help Win the War

Sausage is FOOD POWER!

FOOD POWER BUILDS MAN POWER to do a war winning job. Eat for Food Power because the "U. S. Wants Us Strong." Follow Uncle Sam's Nutrition Program. Every day eat meat, poultry or fish, fruit, vegetables, bread, cereal, milk, cheese, butter or other spreads. These foods contain Food Power . . . and sausage and SKINLESS frankfurters are concentrated meat foods that are delicious and good for you. They contain vitamins, complete proteins, carbohydrates and minerals. 100% edible . . . no waste . . . easy to fix . . . help meal planning.

THERE ARE MANY KINDS OF SAUSAGE, SKINLESS frankfurters and wieners. Each with its own appetizing flavor and goodness in sandwiches, cold and hot meals. Leading packers now protect the food value and flavor of sausage in clear, sparkling "VISKING" casings . . . a cellulose covering you'll recognize instantly. However, the "VISKING" casings are removed from SKINLESS frankfurters and wieners. The surface you see is formed by the wiener itself in the smoking process.

YOUR DEALER KNOWS SAUSAGE, SKINLESS frankfurters and wieners. His stock includes many kinds and brands to fit your needs. Buy wisely so that your meals will always have "Food Power."

THE VISKING CORPORATION • 6733 WEST 65TH STREET, CHICAGO, ILLINOIS

"VISKING" is the registered trade mark of The Visking Corporation   Copyright 1942, The Visking Corporation

JOHN BULL March 12 1955

YOU won't find this family going without a meal if they can help it. Certainly not the one at the end of the day! So, as you can see, they are a thoroughly healthy, contented bunch. With one of those sensible mothers who knows the more her family enjoy a meal the more good it does them.

Home to that good meal they need!

4 out of 6 women know how to make a good meal wonderful

Serve Batchelors Peas! Serve them with beef, or lamb, or pork. Serve them with fish. Have them in casseroles. In salads. Never be without Batchelors Peas. And why Batchelors, you ask? Simply because they're *always* nicer. And so say 4 out of 6 women!*

*A nation-wide survey showed that of all women who named their favourite brand of peas, 4 out of 6 named Batchelors.

Batchelors PEAS

make a good meal **WONDERFUL**

BPP16/89
44

1950s Batchelors Advert

Yes, that's right, mum's fed up of looking after you lot so it's nothing but peas from now on.

**1950s
National
Confectioners
Association Advert**

Personally, I use
up my 'Can Do'
sitting in front of
EastEnders, but it's
good to know I'm
replacing lost
energy and not just
stuffing my face
with Haribo.

1950s Cynamid Advert

This child doesn't look convinced by the pesticide-covered juice. Although maybe she's just mesmerised by her mother's magnificent eyebrows.

How chemistry is saving your orange juice!

Last summer an invasion of the Mediterranean Fruit Fly threatened to destroy Florida's huge citrus crop. Prompt action in spraying thousands of acres with malathion, the remarkably versatile insecticide developed by American Cyanamid Company, is achieving control. As a result, millions of dollars worth of citrus fruits and juices are being saved for America's breakfast table! Here is a dramatic example of how Cyanamid's chemical developments are helping the farmer protect and increase our nation's crops—to serve and conserve in making the fullest possible use of the country's agricultural resources. AMERICAN CYANAMID COMPANY, 30 Rockefeller Plaza, New York 20, N. Y.

CYANAMID

**1900s
Beecham's Advert**

All this eating can play havoc with a girl's digestion. But never fear, Beecham's laxatives will sort things out, leaving you with that attractive 'I've been to the loo twice already today' look.

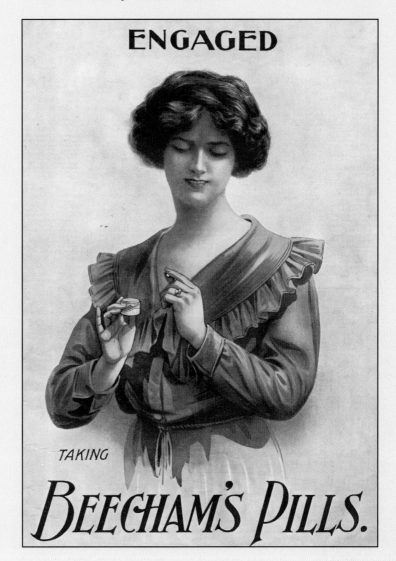

Miracle cures

Feeling a bit down in the dumps? Lacking in vital energy? Then look no further than your nearest plug socket. Yes, back when domestic electricity was new and exciting, consumers were clamouring to buy the latest belt, brush or appliance that would provide them with the revitalising wake-up call of an electric shock. Strange but true. Still, it makes a change from yeast.

But perhaps the greatest example of gullibility seen in these miracle cures is whoever seriously believed that the horse exercise machine was an innocent home work-out …

1880s
Dr Scott's Advert

No need to backcomb your hair with this little beauty; use the electric brush and watch your hair stand on end.

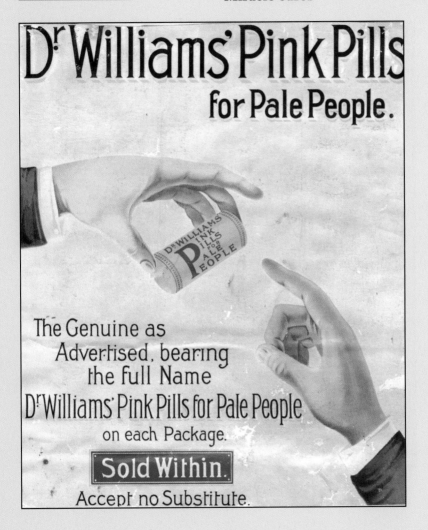

Dr Williams' Pink Pills for Pale People.

The Genuine as Advertised, bearing the full Name Dr Williams' Pink Pills for Pale People on each Package.

Sold Within.

Accept no Substitute.

**1890s
Dr Williams
Advert**

Dr Williams is onto a winner here: invent a mysterious product, market it to a bizarrely specific group of people and – most important of all – keep very quiet about what it's actually supposed to do.

**1890s
Page Woodcock's
Advert**

'Oh, this is so
exciting, having my
portrait painted …
What did you say
I'll be advertising
again?'

HARNESS' EYE BATTERY

(PATENTED).

THE "WONDER CURE" OF THE 19th CENTURY.

A MARVELLOUS INVENTION.

AWAY WITH
EYE-GLASSES
AND
EYE LOTIONS.

Away with Leeching,
Bleeding, and
Surgical Operations.

PRICE
12s. 6d.
POST FREE.

PRICE
12s. 6d.
POST FREE.

By the use of this simple instrument, all the horrible experiences of Leeching, Bleeding, and Surgical Operations are entirely obviated.

A NEW and PAINLESS method of promptly curing all diseases of the Eye, and defective eyesight. Call at 52, **OXFORD STREET, LONDON, W.,** and test the instrument for yourself, free of charge.

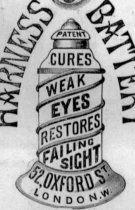

HARNESS' BATTERY

PATENT
CURES
WEAK
EYES
RESTORES
FAILING
SIGHT
52, OXFORD ST.
LONDON. W.

REDUCED FAC-SIMILE OF HARNESS' EYE-BATTERY.
WILL LAST FOR EVER

HARNESS' EYE BATTERY is perfectly safe to use, even by children of tender years, the application being entirely under the patient's control.

HARNESS' EYE BATTERY, in addition to PREVENTING and CURING DISEASES OF THE EYE, will cure asthenopia, and **POSITIVELY RESTORES WEAKNESS OF VISION,** whether resulting from advancing age, or from that general nervous prostration which prejudicially affects the optic nerve. It also speedily **CURES SPECKS BEFORE THE EYES** (*Muscæ Volitantes*), so generally complained of by those suffering from early excesses and in a low and nervous state. Such patients will find in HARNESS' EYE BATTERY an absolute remedy for the malady, which is a real and not, as supposed, an imaginary one, and shows undoubted local manifestation of a debilitated state.

PAMPHLET POST-FREE.

EYES
SUCCESSFULLY
TREATED.

HARNESS' EYE BATTERY, is admitted to exercise a rapid influence upon the complex system of nerves, blood-vessels, fluids, and membranes constituting the most wonderful of Nature's mysterious mechanisms. Almost every disease of the eye can now be successfully treated by the systematic use (according to directions) of HARNESS' EYE BATTERY, which can be applied at any time, as is sufficiently portable to be conveniently carried in the pocket, and may be used by any person from infancy to old age, with perfect safety.

Stated simply, this is a system of curing diseases and weakness of the eye, and restoring normal acuteness of vision by assisting Nature, through influencing the circulatory functions to convey to the affected region a sufficient supply of healthy blood, and thus to annihilate the morbid and stagnant conditions which foster and maintain disease.

HARNESS' EYE BATTERY is sent, carefully packed, with directions for using it, post-free, on receipt of 12s. 6d.

The Medical Battery Co., Ld., **52, OXFORD St., LONDON, W.**

**1890s
Harness Advert**

No more sticking leeches on your eyes. In that case, even an eye battery sounds like a good idea.

**1890s
Brain Salt Advert**

The Pro-Plus for the 19th-century student – Brain Salt promises a certain cure for 'excessive study'. Another is *Jeremy Kyle*.

HORSE EXERCISE AT HOME.

By Royal Letters Patent

Vigor's Horse-Action Saddle

PERSONALLY ORDERED BY H. R. H. THE PRINCESS OF WALES.

Her Excellency the Countess of Aberdeen *writes:* "That the Saddle has given her complete satisfaction."

The ADVANTAGES of this UNIQUE SUBSTITUTE for Horse-Riding are:

It promotes health in the same degree that Horse-Riding does.

It invigorates the system by bringing all the **VITAL ORGANS** into **INSPIRITING ACTION.**

It acts directly upon the **CIRCULATION,** and prevents **STAGNATION OF THE LIVER.**

It is a complete cure for **OBESITY, HYSTERIA,** and **GOUT.**

LANCET :—"Both the expense and difficulty of riding on a live horse are avoided. The invention is very ingenious."

FIELD :—"We have had an opportunity of trying one of the VIGOR's Horse-Action Saddles, and found it very like that of riding on a horse; the same muscles are brought into play as when riding."

WORLD :—"It is good for the figure, good for the complexion, and especially good for the health."

TROT. CANTER. & GALLOP.

VIGOR   LONDON

PARTICULARS, TESTIMONIALS, and **PRESS OPINIONS POST FREE.**

Vigor & Co. 21, Baker St, London.

**1890s
Vigor & Co. Advert**

Ahem. It seems the Countess of Aberdeen is 'completely satisfied' by her horse-action saddle. Lucky her.

1900s
Dr McLaughlin
Co. Advert

This belt apparently provides 'courage'. Or maybe others are just scared by the constant buzz emanating from your middle.

ELECTRICITY VICTORIOUS

Amazing Results with Electrical Treatment in the Home.

INFINITE JOY OF HEALTH

Although universally accepted as being the most powerful curative agent in existence, many sufferers have yet to learn of the extraordinary powers of the new treatment by which curative, life-giving, and revitalising Electricity can now be applied in the home by means of simple appliances, which even a child can manipulate.

The wonderful "AJAX" Dry-Cell Body Batteries infuse new life and energy into your weakened body; they drive out pains and aches, and restore your bodily functions to a perfectly healthy condition.

A SCIENTIFIC FACT

The reason why is very simple; the motive power of the human machinery is Electricity, and when through excessive strain, overwork, or chronic complaints this natural strength has been overdrawn upon, the functions get out of gear, and suffering is the result; you become but a shadow of your former self, weak and debilitated. But give back to your body what it has lost, and so surely as an electric bell starts ringing immediately you press the button, if the CURRENT IS THERE, so will you recover health, strength and well-being if you will renew your store of Electricity to its proper level. If you overdraw your account at the bank the matter is remedied by supplying fresh funds. That is exactly the point: refill your overdrawn system with its life power and all will be well again.

All the greatest scientists endorse our contention that Electricity is the very life of the human body, and therefore you must investigate this unfailing means of regaining the infinite joy of vigorous, robust health.

80 PAGES BRIMFUL OF KNOWLEDGE

That is our booklet, entitled "Electricity the Road to Health." Write for it at once, TO-DAY, and you will learn how a host of complaints are successfully overcome; Weakness in all its forms is vanquished; Rheumatic, Neuralgic, and every other pain dispelled for ever; Indigestion, Constipation, Liver, Kidney, and Bladder troubles cured, never to return; Brain-fag, and all nervous complaints completely eliminated. This small book will cost you nothing, but may be worth a fortune to you. Write for it now, whilst you have it in mind, or call if possible at the Institute, when in a personal consultation you will be told exactly what can be done for you, free of charge, and get a free test and examination of the appliances. Do not "Put off"; call or write at once for full particulars. AJAX LD.

THE BRITISH ELECTRIC INSTITUTE (Dept. 163), 25 Holborn Viaduct, LONDON, E.C.1

1910s
Ajax Advert

This Ajax battery cures constipation – not a huge surprise. You try not going when you're being electrocuted.

1918
Formamint Advert

The flu epidemic of 1918 killed millions, but
clearly not those sucking Formamint!

NEURASTHENIA CURED BY ELECTRICITY.

WONDERFUL CURES OF NERVE WEAKNESS, DEBILITY, AND NERVOUS DYSPEPSIA.

TO-DAY, the conditions of life are causing a serious increase in Neurasthenia and other nervous and Functional disorders.

The symptoms of Neurasthenia are many and varied. They are mainly mental or nervous, and often the victim is quite unaware of the fact that he or she is travelling rapidly towards Nervous Exhaustion and Nervous Prostration.

HAVE YOU ANY OF THESE SYMPTOMS ?

Are you Nervous, Timid, or Indecisive ?

Do you lack Self-Confidence ?

Do you dread Open or Closed Spaces ?

Are you wanting in Will Power ?

Are you "Fidgety," Restless, or Sleepless ?

Do you Blush or Turn Pale readily ?

Do you shrink from Strange Company ?

Are you subject to Sudden Impulses ?

Do you crave for Stimulants or Drugs ?

If so, you can safely assume that you are suffering from Neurasthenia. The Neurasthenic also often suffer from **Indigestion, Liver Troubles, Constipation, Palpitation, Loss of Appetite, Excess of Appetite,** and a host of other disorders due to faulty functioning of various organs. Electricity is the only force that naturally supplies this deficiency of Nerve Force, and restores tone to the whole nervous system.

The greatest neurologists, including Erb, Beard, Loeb, and hundreds of the foremost medical thinkers, now agree that electrical treatment, skilfully and scientifically directed, will revitalise depleted nerve centres (as in

ARE YOU NERVOUS LIKE THIS ?

If so, Curative Electricity will put you right. The Pulvermacher Appliances are the only inventions for the administration of curative electricity, endorsed by over fifty leading Doctors and by the official Academy of Medicine in Paris.

neurasthenia, debility, and nervous dyspepsia), restore sound digestion, invigorate the circulation, and increase the daily and necessary elimination of the waste products that, if uneliminated, are the greatest source of all diseases.

To-day you can be

CURED IN YOUR OWN HOME BY ELECTRICITY

by simply wearing the Pulvermacher appliances, which are light, easy, and comfortable to wear. They give no shock, but all the time they are being worn they supply the nerve centres with a continuous flow of electricity, naturally stimulate the circulation of the blood and increase nerve nutrition.

This is the natural and physiological treatment of Neurasthenia, which drug treatments can never cure. The Pulvermacher Treatment has cured the most obstinate cases of Neurasthenia and Nervous Disorders when all other methods have failed. If you are suffering from any form of Nerve Trouble, or if you have any of the symptoms as here described, write to-day for a book that may well prove of incalculable health value to you, yet it costs you nothing. It is entitled "Guide to Health and Strength," and will be sent post free.

Those who can call personally are cordially invited to do so, when a consultation on their health trouble may be secured absolutely free of charge and without obligation between the hours of 10.0 and 5.30 daily.

─FREE COUPON─

By posting this **FREE FORM TO-DAY** you will receive the "**Guide to Health and Strength.**" You place yourself under no obligation by applying for this Book and particulars of the Pulvermacher Appliances.

Name...

Address...

....

Post to the Superintendent, Pulvermacher Electrological Institute, Ltd., 81, Vulcan House, 56, Ludgate Hill, London, E.C. 4.   *The Sphere, January 25, 1919*

1920
Pulvermacher Electrological Institute Advert

Don't waste your time being scared of the car, old guy – you're stood next to Lightbulb Man!

1920s
Dr West's Advert

Jim was doing well to keep his relaxed and easy manner when faced with the terror of sogginess.

Impossible to keep teeth white unless your brush is *anti-soggy!*

YOU'VE NOTICED IT YOURSELF. Very few people you see have really white—sparkling-white teeth. All of them probably realize the importance of attractive teeth. All of them probably brush their teeth regularly. But almost certainly, most of them make one fatal mistake. They use brushes that grow flabby and limp when wet.

They waste their time with *soggy* brushes—brushes that are worn-out or cheap or made with a poor grade of bristles. And such *soggy* brushes cannot possibly keep teeth really clean. If you want brilliant-white, attractive teeth, act today. Throw away your *soggy* toothbrush. Get one of the two *anti-soggy* brushes described below.

New! Dr. West's Economy brush

ANTI-SOGGY! Now a medium-priced brush that really keeps teeth white! An achievement in manufacturing possible only to the world's foremost makers of toothbrushes. You get the famous DR. WEST'S design in this new *Economy* brush. It cleans every surface, every crevice. And this remarkable brush is *anti-soggy*. It gives you the greatest protection against sogginess, the greatest cleansing power ever offered at this price. High grade, selected bristles are used in making it. (These bristles are *not*, however, water-proofed.) Comes sterilized and sealed. In six beautiful colors. **29¢** MADE IN U.S.A.

Copr. 1934 by W. B. M. Co.

Dr. West's famous Water-proofed brush

WATER-PROOFED AGAINST SOGGINESS! The most widely used, most effective toothbrush offered for sale today. Gives 60% better results in keeping teeth brilliant-white, in ease and quickness of cleansing. It is the only toothbrush *water-proofed* against sogginess. It is made of the world's costliest bristles—hand selected. And these splendid bristles are harmlessly water-proofed. They cannot grow soggy when wet. Small in size, correct in design, it cleans every surface, every crevice. It is the only brush that is sold surgically sterile—sealed germ-proof in glass. In ten gem-like colors. **50¢** MADE IN U.S.A.

TO BE SURE OF HAVING WHITE, ATTRACTIVE TEETH ALSO DO THIS: USE DR. WEST'S QUICK-CLEANSING TOOTH PASTE — ABSOLUTELY SAFE, UNUSUALLY EFFECTIVE

The PASSING SHOW, July 15, 1933   (Supplement)

Don't You Feel Well Mummy?

How Can You Tell Them You Feel

EXHAUSTED NERVY, HEADACHY, WEAK, DYSPEPTIC, LISTLESS, Thoroughly RUN-DOWN & OUT OF SORTS?

THEY know "something" is wrong—but they don't realise how ill you feel! They don't know how you WEAR YOURSELF OUT looking after them, how the daily tasks seem to sap every ounce of your vitality, how their noise and chatter makes your head ache and throb—tears your nerves to shreds! But we know how the cares of motherhood wear down the strongest system. We know how you feel—that is why we tell you to take "Yeast-Vite" Brand Tonic Tablets.

TAKE 2 OR 3 YEAST-VITE TABLETS AND FEEL FIT AND FRESH IN A FEW MINUTES

—Why continue to be agonised by Terrible Headaches, Niggling Nerve Pains, Black Depression, and Heavy-Limbed Lassitude?

—Why go on denying yourself the Gift of Sound Digestion, Steady Nerves and Unflagging Energy when you can experience the benefit of this marvellous Lightning PICK-ME-UP?

Yeast-Vite has conquered. It has come as a marvel of relief to Tired, Exhausted mothers. It has restored Brightness to the Eye and Youthful Bloom to Pale, Wan Cheeks. It has given Energy to men where before was the hopeless, listless anguish of Nagging Headaches and Worn-out Nerves.

"Yeast-Vite" regulates the action of the Digestive Tract. It relieves and banishes Dyspepsia. And in cases of Anæmia, Sleeplessness, Stomach Troubles, and Constipation it works absolute wonders.

For "Yeast-Vite" supplies to your body just those essential elements of well-being which a Run-down and Pain-racked system needs. In this accurate Scientific Combination of Pure Medicinal Yeast (Saccharomycetis Cerevisiae), Valuable Vitamins and other Tonic Ingredients is a concentrated source of New Life, New Health and Vigorous Vitality for YOU.

YOUR QUICK-HEALTH TIME-TABLE

FROM	TO	TIME
NERVE PAINS	Glorious Relief	In 5/15 MINS.
HEADACHES	Deliverance	In 5/15 MINS.
LASSITUDE	Vim and Vigour	In 10/20 MINS.
DEPRESSION	Buoyant Energy	In 10/20 MINS.
"NERVES"	Steadiness	In 10/90 MINS.
INDIGESTION	Keen Appetite	In 15/30 MINS.
EXHAUSTION	Animation	In 15/30 MINS.
SLEEPLESSNESS	Calm Repose	In 30/60 MINS.
RHEUMATISM	Pain Relief	In 24 HOURS
CONSTIPATION	Regularity	In 36 HOURS
IMPURE BLOOD	Purification	In 36 HOURS

NO CURE — NO PAY

Simply obtain a 1/3 bottle of "YEAST-VITE" Brand Quick-Tonic Tablets from any Chemist. Try the treatment at our risk, and if you are not THOROUGHLY CONVINCED of the WONDERFUL POWER PERFECT SAFETY, and TONIC PROPERTIES of "YEAST-VITE," return the empty carton to Irving's Yeast-Vite Ltd., Watford, and your money will be refunded in full.

Yeast-Vite
BRAND

Quick-Tonic Tablets. All Chemists, 3d., 6d., 1/3, 3/- & 5/-

1930s YeastVite Advert

Oh no, thoroughly run-down? How rotten! What you need is YeastVite, a certain cure for annoying children.

1930s Fleischmann Advert

'It's difficult to do your work and keep pleasant'. How true, Jones, how true.

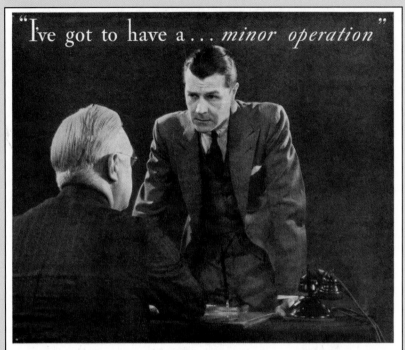

"I've got to have a... *minor operation*"

More serious than most men realize... the troubles caused by harsh toilet tissue

IN nearly every business organization a surprisingly large percentage of the employees are suffering from rectal trouble.

This fact is well known to companies that require physical examinations of their personnel. Yet even these same concerns are frequently negligent in providing equipment that will safeguard the health of their employees.

Harsh toilet tissue, for instance.

Any physician will tell you that mucous membrane can be seriously inflamed by the use of harsh or chemically impure toilet tissue.

Some specialists estimate that 65 per cent of all men and women at middle age suffer from troubles caused or aggravated by inferior toilet tissue.

Protection from rectal illness is just as important in the home as in business. Fortunately, women are more careful in matters of this kind than men. Already millions of homes are equipped with ScotTissue or Waldorf—the tissues that doctors and hospitals recommend.

Extremely soft, cloth-like and absorbent, these safety tissues cannot harm the most sensitive skin. They are chemically pure, contain no harsh irritants.

Be safe . . . at home, at work. Insist on Scot-Tissue or Waldorf. Scott Paper Company, Chester, Pa. In Canada, Scott Paper Company, Ltd., Toronto, Ontario.

SCOTTISSUE, *an extremely soft, pure white, absorbent roll containing 1,000 sheets*

2 for 25¢
Price for U. S. only

Soft as old Linen

ScotTissue
The absorbent soft white toilet tissue
Scott Paper Company

Waldorf
A Scott Tissue

WALDORF, *soft and absorbent, yet inexpensive*
Now 6¢ a roll
Price for U. S. only

Stores displaying this sign [Featured at this store! HEALTH PRODUCTS It will pay you to buy in quantities] are featuring Health Products during June and July

**1930s
J. W. Simpson
Advert**

... and for our next product, magic beans!

NOW she is *immune* from 'Flu, Colds or any epidemic for 12 months because she is wearing the Simpson Iodine Locket

Whilst worn, the Iodine is constantly breathed into the system through the skin pores for 12 months (the life of the Locket).

Men wear the Locket in the vest pocket.

More than 2,500,000 wearers have in this way been kept free from 'Flu, Colds, Catarrh and Rheumatism.

This is Mr. J. W. Simpson, Chemist, the Iodine Specialist, Inventor of the "IODOLOK" Iodine Locket.

The Locket is sold by all Chemists, 1/9 each, 3 for 4/6. But see the name and the word "IODOLOK" embossed in gold on the Locket, as there are some cheap imitations about.

J. W. SIMPSON (CHEMIST) LTD., ALDWYCH HOUSE, LONDON, W.C.2

27

A woman's work is always fun

Before the evil cloud of feminism cast its shadow over so many happy homes, encouraging women to leave their housework and wear dungarees instead, little ladies the world over were busy having fun washing up and vacuuming. They liked nothing more than to receive a household appliance for Christmas and serve up a delicious meal of canned soup to their hungry husbands. Occasionally, they even troubled their pretty little heads with the world of work, where they had much fun typing up clever men's business (goodness knows what it was all about, but when their typewriters were so nice and colourful, who cared?)

**1920s
Lux Advert**

Moral of the story:
wash your pants or
risk the sack.

A WARNING

to girls who work in offices

Nervous strain increases perspiration—
don't run the risk of "undie odor"

Please do not expect employers
or even office mates to warn you of this
hard-to-forgive offense.

Girls who work in offices are so apt to
run the risk of unpleasant "undie odor."
Naturally so, because everybody per-
spires more under nervous tension.
And underthings are constantly ab-
sorbing perspiration acids and odors.
Others notice this before you do.

Don't take chances that may spoil
your business success. There is one
sure way to *know* you're fresh and
sweet. Lux removes "undie odor" *completely*, yet so gently that colors and
fabrics are never harmed.

It's delightfully easy to Lux your
lingerie and stockings after *every* wearing. Then you avoid all embarrass-
ment, all risk of offending. This dainty
habit takes only 4 minutes, or less!

Try Lux FREE! Try this wonderful care for
your lingerie, at our expense. Just send us your
name and address, and by return mail you will
receive a full-sized package of Lux *free*. Write
today to Lever Brothers Company, Dept.
BX-5, Cambridge, Massachusetts.

Risking her job?

Clever, efficient, her loyalty and hard
work are surely appreciated. Yet this
offense is too serious—no one could
overlook it. If only some one could
warn her that she is risking her job!

LUX

Pretty Hands
Lux in the DISHPAN
leaves hands soft, snow-
white. Costs only 1 c a day!

LUX for underthings—

keeps them like new in spite of frequent washing

1930s
Kellogg's Advert

Yes, and the more comments like that a husband makes, the more likely he is to go to work in dirty socks.

**1930s
Lux Advert**

Got that? Men can't fall in love with a woman
who offends!

**1930s
Campbell Advert**

Clever?! For a start she's serving soup on a plate, which is never a good idea.

1936
Listerine Advert

Poor old stinky Edna. Can you imagine a more horrifying prospect for a woman than being unmarried in her late 20s?

Often a bridesmaid but never a bride

EDNA'S case was really a pathetic one. Like every woman, her primary ambition was to marry. Most of the girls of her set were married—or about to be. Yet not one possessed more grace or charm or loveliness than she.

And as her birthdays crept gradually toward that tragic thirty-mark, marriage seemed farther from her life than ever.

She was often a bridesmaid but never a bride.

* * *

That's the insidious thing about halitosis (unpleasant breath). You, yourself, rarely know when you have it. And even your closest friends won't tell you.

Sometimes, of course, halitosis comes from some deep-seated organic disorder that requires professional advice. But usually—and fortunately—halitosis is only a local condition that yields to the regular use of Listerine as a mouth wash and gargle. It is an interesting thing that this well-known antiseptic that has been in use for years for surgical dressings, possesses these unusual properties as a breath deodorant.

It halts food fermentation in the mouth and leaves the breath sweet, fresh and clean. *Not* by substituting some other odor but by really removing the old one. The Listerine odor itself quickly disappears. So the systematic use of Listerine puts you on the safe and polite side.

Your druggist will supply you with Listerine. He sells lots of it. It has dozens of different uses as a safe antiseptic and has been trusted as such for half a century. Remember, Listerine is as safe as it is effective. Lambert Pharmacal Company, St. Louis, Mo.

THE HIT OF PALM BEACH

Fits into purse, keeps powder, lipstick and other cosmetics in one place.

This smart Moire Cosmetic Bag **FREE** →
WITH PURCHASE OF LARGE SIZE LISTERINE
This offer good in U.S.A. only

At your druggist's while they last

1950s
Horlicks Advert

Come-hither Horlicks? Well it's certainly a lot
easier than stockings and suspenders...

**1940s
Climax Advert**

Now she has her Climax, washday's her favourite day of the week. Funny that.

1952
Macleans Advert

Good, because if
not the wedding's
off quicker than
you can say 'Is that
a lump of spinach
between your
grotty teeth?'

1940s
Tern Advert

And what makes a perfect man? Someone who pretends to love getting another boring shirt for his birthday?

To Gladden Hearts and *Lighten* Labor

DOWMETAL···THE WORLD'S LIGHTEST STRUCTURAL ALLOY

Almost a score of years ago Dow undertook to produce American made magnesium alloys—the metal that is a full third lighter than aluminum.

Then, and through the years, Dow looked forward to the day when the startling lightness of this metal would make a myriad of tasks easier for mankind.

First to take advantage of Dowmetal was the aviation industry where its unique lightness combined with strength is of untold value.

Gradually it found acceptance in industry—adding speed to machine parts, cutting power costs, aiding transportation and speeding manual operations.

Finally, a year ago, Dowmetal entered the household appliance field through its adoption by The Hoover

Company for the famous Hoover One Fifty Cleaning Ensemble. So audible has been customer enthusiasm for the amazing lightness of that product that Hoover designers determined to incorporate this feature in the just-announced lower priced Hoover Model 25.

Obviously, Dow has long since overcome those problems of production which stood in its developmental period as economic barriers to wider use. Moreover, recent advances in fabrication, notably high speed die-casting, enable users of Dowmetal to adapt it to their production methods on a close-cost basis.

Thus, the ambition for Dowmetal is now realized. It is serving industry in an ever broadening capacity and finding its way into the homes of people—to gladden their hearts and lighten their labors.

DOW

CHEMICALS INDISPENSABLE TO INDUSTRY

THE DOW CHEMICAL COMPANY, MIDLAND, MICHIGAN

Branch Sales Offices: 30 Rockefeller Plaza, New York City • Second and Madison Streets, St. Louis • 135 South La Salle Street, Chicago

1950s Dow Advert

Seconds after the blindfold came off, the vacuum cleaner was wrapped around Mr Smith's head.

**1950s
Sky-line Advert**

Lucky girl indeed! Although any woman this attached to her knives is probably in anger management classes.

If your husband ever finds out

you're not "store-testing" for fresher coffee...

...if he discovers you're
still taking chances
on getting flat, stale coffee
...woe be unto you!
For today
there's a sure
and certain way
to test for freshness
<u>before</u> you buy

Here's how easy it is to be sure of fresher coffee

Look for the "Dome Top" Can of Chase & Sanborn. That firm, rounded top shows it's packed *under pressure*, fresh from the oven.

Just do this:

Press your thumbs against the dome top *before* you buy. If it's firm, it's fresh. If the top clicks, pressure's gone—take another. It's the one way to get the freshest coffee ever packed.

No other can lets you test!

You can't test an ordinary flat top can. Some are "leakers" that have let air in to steal freshness. But all flat top cans look alike. You can't tell which are good and which are stale.

Here's the payoff!

Sure as you pour a cup, they'll want more! For Chase & Sanborn is a glorious blend of more expensive coffees . . . brought to you *fresher*. No wonder Chase & Sanborn pays a flavor dividend you won't find in any other coffee!

"PRESSURE PACKED"

REGULAR GRIND

PRESSURE PACKED
Chase & Sanborn
COFFEE

Chase & Sanborn

103

**1950s
Chase & Sanborn
Advert**

And if he catches
you using tea bags
instead of loose,
he'll lock you in
the cupboard for
a week.

**1950
IBM Advert**

If this is really her idea of a perfect day, then she is on some serious medication.

ISN'T GEORGE SWEET... Leaving it there for me to find. He knew how I hated our old sink. And now this heavenly surprise. Leisure of all things. Nothing but the best for George. It looks so right and is so sensible. That ultra-deep bowl. Positively masses of draining board. And such a wonderful white. Obviously designed by a woman. But it was bought by my George. Bless him! IN WHITE OR COLOURED VITREOUS ENAMEL. FROM £6.6.0 OR STAINLESS STEEL (FITTINGS EXTRA). MADE FOR LEISURE OR OTHER CABINETS.

LEISURE SINKS MADE BY **ALLIED IRONFOUNDERS**

Allied Ironfounders LEISURE
Leisure Works, Long Eaton, Notts.

NAME

ADDRESS

HWLSt/11

SHOWROOMS: 149 REGENT STREET, LONDON W1

**1960s
Allied
Ironfounders
Advert**

I'm not sure George is so confident about his gift – looks like he's poised for a quick exit through the window in case she throws it at him.

Acknowledgements

All the images used in this book were provided by the Advertising Archives, except p37, which was kindly supplied by Minnie Fingerhut. Thanks to the companies and products featured for permission to reproduce their adverts. Particular credits are as follows:

p58 reproduced by kind permission of White Castle System, Inc., All Rights Reserved. p61 reproduced by kind permission of the National Confectioners Association.

This edition first published in 2008 by New Holland Publishers (UK) Ltd
London • Cape Town • Sydney • Auckland
www.newhollandpublishers.com

10 9 8 7 6 5 4 3 2 1

Garfield House, 86–88 Edgware Road, London W2 2EA, UK
80 McKenzie Street, Cape Town 8001, South Africa
Unit 1, 66 Gibbes Street, Chatswood, NSW 2067, Australia
218 Lake Road, Northcote, Auckland, New Zealand

ISBN: 978 1 84773 320 7

Publishing Director: Rosemary Wilkinson
Senior Editor: Kate Parker
Cover design: Ken Griffiths
Design: Zoë Mellors
Production: Melanie Dowland

A hardback edition of this book was first published in 2007 as *What The Doctor Smokes*.

Reproduction by Modern Age Repro House Ltd, Hong Kong
Printed and bound by Craft Print International Pte Ltd, Singapore